GW01465845

DINOSAURS

Written by Amanda Ronan and Chris Madsen
Illustrated by James Field

Henderson Publishing
Woodbridge, England

Dinosaurs were a group of reptiles (animals that were cold-blooded and had a backbone), with scaly skin, and they laid eggs. They lived on Earth from about 240 to 65 million years ago, a total of 175 million years. That is 87 times longer than the 2 million years that we believe human beings have lived.

Why 'Dinosaur'?

Dinosaurs were first called 'dinosaur' in 1841 by Dr Richard Owen. It means 'terrible lizard' in Greek.

Different Types

There were many different sorts of dinosaur, many were gigantic, and some were tiny, the size of a chicken. Scientists believe they divided into two different groups, the lizard-hipped dinosaurs (like **Brontosaurus**) and the bird-hipped dinosaurs (like **Iguanodon**). These groups had very different skeletons.

Meat or Vegetables?

Some dinosaurs had deadly slashing teeth and claws which they used to kill, and eat other reptiles. Other dinosaurs were gentle, peaceful plant eaters.

Where did they Live?

We have found dinosaur remains almost everywhere we have looked. When dinosaurs began, most of the world's land was in one big lump, called Pangaea. This then split into three big pieces, which were N. America plus Europe, Africa plus S. America, and Australia plus Antarctica. India broke off from between Africa and Antarctica and moved north towards Asia. By the time the dinosaurs became extinct, Africa and South America had come apart but Europe and America were still joined, even then.

Afloat on Huge Rafts

As the continents broke up, the dinosaurs were carried with them. This is why we find remains of very similar kinds in Europe and N. America. One early kind has even turned up in S. Africa, India, and Antarctica!

Colour

No one knows the true colour of the dinosaurs, although they are often shown as brightly coloured. Scientists are constantly changing their ideas about dinosaurs as new information is found.

DISCOVERING DINOSAURS

Most of what we have learned has come from fossils. A fossil is usually the remains of a plant or animal, which has been turned into stone over millions of years. By studying them and comparing them to things living today, scientists have given us a picture of what the Earth was like millions of years ago.

How are Fossils Made?

When a dinosaur died, the soft parts of its body either rotted away, or were eaten by other hungry animals. Then, over time, its skeleton became buried by grains of dust and dirt called sediment. As the bones became deeper and deeper, the sediment above got so squashed that it became rock, and the bones hardened to stone — it became fossilized.

All Sorts of Fossils

Not all fossils are bones. Tracks and footprints have been found, also shells, teeth, horns, skin, hair, nests and even eggs. From this we know that dinosaurs laid eggs and brought food to their young, just as birds do today. In fact, birds are the nearest relations to dinosaurs.

Where are Fossils Found?

Fossils are mostly buried deep underground, and so the easiest way to find them is to look at places where the rock has been split, or worn away: cliffs at the seaside, or where a river or stream cuts deeply into the ground.

The Age of Rock

Rocks lie in layers, and so a fossil found in rock will be as old as the rock in which it is found. The deepest gorge in the Earth's surface is the Grand Canyon in North America. Scientists have learnt much about the Earth's past from the 2000 million years of rock layers and fossil history present there.

An Early Puzzle

Until a few years before dinosaur bones first came to light, people believed that the world was only about 6000 years old. This had been worked out from the Bible, and it made it very difficult for people to understand what fossils were!

Some Extinct Theories

Before people understood how old the Earth was, they came up with some ideas about fossils that seem very funny to us now. One explanation was that they were put there by the devil to confuse people, and another was that they were the remains of animals that had been drowned in the Flood when Noah escaped in his ark. The nearest explanation to the truth was the suggestion that fossils were mistakes that God made while he was creating all the animals.

Giants

For a while, dinosaur bones were seen as evidence that giants once lived on Earth.

If rock is soft, the fossils can be dug out carefully. But if it is very hard scientists chip around it slowly. If the bone is very fragile, it can be treated with liquid plastic while still in the rock, to make it stronger. If a bone is fractured or broken, it can be given a plastercast — just like when you have a broken arm or leg!

Once removed, the bones are taken to a museum, where they are cleaned, either in an acid bath, or they are shaken in a special way so that the loose grains of rock fall away. The bones can be repaired with glue or plaster of Paris, and varnished with a sort of plastic to protect them. There are often bones missing from the skeleton, so scientists look at other fossils and work out what the missing bones would have looked like, and make copies.

Jigsaw

Many stout metal bars and cables are needed to support the huge dinosaur skeleton that is recreated. From skeletons, experts have worked out what the dinosaurs really looked like, and how they behaved. The skeleton of **Coelophysis** for example, was found complete, and we know that it ran quickly as it has thin light bones. **Diplodocus** has big strong bones, so it was a very slow-moving, big animal.

First Bone

The first bone was found over 300 years ago. In 1677 Dr Robert Plot, Professor of Chemistry at Oxford University, described a piece of a thigh bone which, although it is now lost, seems to have been part of a **Megalosaur.** He did his best to make sense of this and other fossils and teeth that people gave him, but became very confused because some had come from churchyards! This isn't surprising, really, because graveyards are places where people often dig holes, but Dr Plot took it to mean that they were the bones of long-ago giant men or women.

A Great Team

Gideon Mantell was a doctor whose hobby was fossil-hunting, and his wife, Mary Ann, was just as keen. In 1822, she found a strange-looking tooth in a rockpile. Three years later, after finding more teeth and bones and doing a lot of detective work, Dr Mantell named his discovery **Iguanodon,** meaning 'iguana tooth'.

HOW LIFE BEGAN

The world is changing all the time, it has not always been the same as it is today. Thousands of millions of years ago, the Earth was covered in molten rock and its heat was so great that it boiled all the water into steam, making great clouds of gases. Nothing could breathe or live there.

The Great Rains

Then the Earth slowly cooled down, and it rained, without stopping, for millions of years. This rain made the oceans and seas. When the rains stopped, the sun broke through the clouds and life began in the seas. The first plants were **algae** and the first tiny animals were **protozoa.** A few million years later, the first sea creatures appeared, such as corals, sponges and jellyfish.

A Variety of Creatures

Shelled animals also evolved in the warm, shallow oceans. There were sea-snails and starfishes, and a great number and variety of now-extinct jointed creatures called **Trilobites.** Other animals with jointed shell-skeletons (arthropods) arose, and grew big and strong.

First Fish

About 450 million years ago, the first fish appeared. They were very different from the fish of today, with bony heads, and were mostly quite small.

Dangerous World

Arthropods today don't grow nearly as big as animals with backbones (vertebrates), but early fishes came into a world already full of big, clawed hunters. There were giant sea-scorpions more than 6 feet long, with huge jagged claws. Many early fishes grew heavy, thick, bony armour to protect them from such fearsome enemies.

Monster Fish

Dinichthys was about 9m long, the same size as a bus, and its jaws had sharp blades about 60cm long!

Rising Land

Around 400 million years ago, the land began to rise, so some of the seaweeds had to adapt to life on land. They were relatives of the mosses and ferns of today, but some were as tall as trees. The first creatures to leave the water for the land were the primitive insects — giant dragonflies as big as birds, such as **Meganeura,** which had a wingspan of 76cm!

ONTO THE LAND

Around 350 million years ago, there began a long stretch of seasonal droughts, when some of the lakes and swamps dried up at certain times of the year. The animals living in these pools had to find a way to exist during these droughts, or they would have died out.

Lungfish
Some fish developed lungs, just like we have, which meant that they could gulp mouthfuls of air when there was no water left.

The Lobefins
Another group of fish developed incredibly strong front and back fins, so strong that they could drag themselves around the land looking for other pools of water. On the way they could breathe air.
Eusthenopteron was a lobefin, the size of a large salmon.

Amphibians

Millions of years passed, and the amphibians evolved. The word 'amphibious' comes from the Greek, meaning 'having a double life', and this is true. They could live both in the water and on land. They needed to swim to keep their skins moist, as they breathe through their skins; because their eggs do not have a waterproof shell, they lay their eggs in water.

Of the modern day amphibians, the frogs, toads, newts and salamanders are probably most like their ancestors, although they are much smaller.

Ichthyostega

One of the first amphibians was called **Ichthyostega,** and was discovered in Greenland. It had lungs and proper legs, with webbed feet. Although it was a four legged animal, it was undoubtedly a good swimmer. It probably fed on the land, eating mostly insects and snails, and was about 90cm long.

THE AMPHIBIANS

As time went by, many different amphibians evolved, and for a while the swamps were filled with them, in fact they ruled the Earth for many millions of years.

How Big?

They ranged in size from 5cm, to Eogyrynus which was 4.5m long. Some had very sharp teeth, and it is known that some large amphibians could eat the small amphibians, whereas the small ones ate insects on land and molluscs, fishes and other water-creatures in the swamps.

Their skins were tougher, which probably meant they could spend more time out of the water without drying up. But they still had to lay their eggs in water, so they stayed around the swamps and pools. They no longer had fins on their tails, and their feet were not as webbed as older amphibians like **Ichthyostega.**

So Far, So Good

For as long as the tropical forests lasted, amphibians were in both of their elements. Their eggs in the water must have been gobbled up by many creatures but this was balanced by the fact that, on land, the adults had hardly any enemies except other amphibians.

Nothing Lasts Forever

The earthquakes and upheavals continued, raising more and more land out of the water. Life became harder for amphibians as they needed to travel further to find water to lay eggs in. At the same time, another kind of four-legged vertebrate was evolving, one with scaly waterproof skin and another talent that freed it from dependence on water.

The Reptile's Secret

The secret to the reptile's success was that it did not need to lay its eggs in water. Amphibians' eggs are small and soft, like frogspawn, and if they are left out of water they dry up and die. Reptiles' eggs have a hard leathery shell. The young reptile inside is fed on yolk until it hatches.

Where Did Reptiles Come From?

Nobody is quite sure which amphibians evolved into reptiles. It is suggested that, one day, a 'missing link' may be found, but it might even be possible that reptiles evolved from fishes quite separately.

THE LAND REPTILES

Reptiles ruled the land for more than 200 years. The earliest known reptiles lived 300 million years ago. Their fossils were found in Nova Scotia, Canada.

Seymouria was one of the first reptiles. It was about 60cm long, and looked quite like an amphibian.

Sails

Different types of reptiles began to appear, such as the fin-backs or sail-backs. Two fossils of fin-backs were found in Texas, **Dimetrodon** and **Edaphosaurus.** They lived 270 million years ago, when it was very hot and dry. The sails on their backs were made of spines covered by skin.

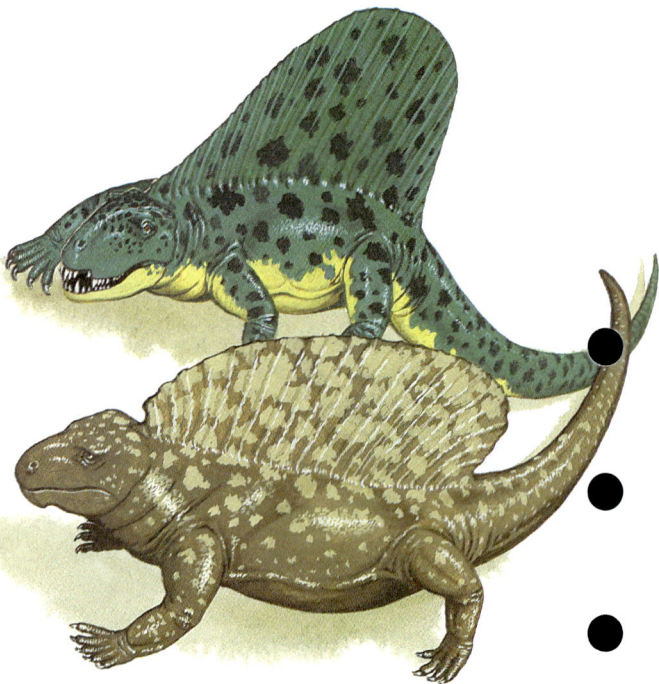

Cold-Blooded

Humans are warm-blooded, our temperature is almost always the same, and is automatically controlled. Reptiles are cold-blooded, which means that the blood temperature will change depending on the sun and air around them. Dinosaurs used their 'sails' like radiators, turning them towards the sun when they wanted to warm up, and away to cool down. That is why we see lizards bask on rocks — to 'soak up' the sun, and so raise their body temperature.

Edaphosaurus was about 2.7m long, and was one of the first animals to learn to eat land plants.

Edaphosaurus bones have been found in both Texas and Czechoslovakia, giving proof that Europe and N. America were joined together when it walked the Earth. **Dimetrodon** was much more agile, and was a meat eater, so probably had to run to catch the smaller amphibians and reptiles. At the highest point, its sail was taller than a man! Dimetrodon's other claim to fame is that it was in fact the largest meat-eater in the reptile group that went on to evolve into mammals.

First and Last Reptiles

Among the earliest of reptiles were the **Rhynchosaurs,** lizard-like creatures that were soon pushed out by the dinosaurs. Curiously, though, they left a single surviving species in the form of the Tuatara, a true living fossil of New Zealand. Turtles also evolved very early and and they, too, seem to have managed to bypass the fate of the great ruling reptiles.

REPTILES AT SEA

About 210 million years ago, three groups of reptiles left the land to go back to live in the sea. Some spent all their time in water, while others were able to come out and lay their eggs on land, as turtles do nowadays. The reptiles which returned to the water could not simply shed their feet and grow fins like their ancestors. They had to go through the slow process of adapting their bodies for swimming by gradually taking on a more streamlined shape, and adapting their fingers and toes until they eventually became like paddles. The largest sea reptile was **Stretosaurus.** A jawbone, found in Britain, was over 3m long!

The Ichthyosaurs

This group were the most fish-like, and they moved quickly through the water by making wavy motions with their strong tails and bodies, like fish do. They even had fins on their backs. In fact, they looked very like dolphins, although they were up to 9m long! They had long beaks, with many sharp teeth for catching fish. The **ichthyosaurs** could not walk on land, so their eggs hatched inside the females and the young were born alive in water. They had to come to the surface of the sea to breathe air, since they had lungs, like dolphins today.

Webbed Feet

While early Ichthyosaurs were being 'reptile-dolphins', another group of early reptiles were living rather like modern seals. These were the **Nothosaurs,** which looked a little like giant newts, with a flattened tail and webbed feet. They reversed the amphibian life-style by hunting in coastal waters and breeding on land. We believe that they were ancestors of **Plesiosaurs.**

The Plesiosaurs

These were slow-moving reptiles, with very long necks and small heads, broad flat bodies and four powerful flippers. They were up to 12m long. The Loch Ness Monster is said to look very like a **plesiosaur,** but they all died out at least 70 million years ago.

GLIDING REPTILES

While reptiles, and then dinosaurs, were roaming the land, a group of gliding reptiles called the **pterosaurs** were masters of the air. They were rather like bats, as they glided, using the winds and air currents to keep them aloft. They came in many sizes, some were no bigger than a sparrow, others had a wing span of 10m or more.

Wings

Pterosaurs did not have feathery wings like birds. Instead the wings were made of a thin layer of skin, stretched along an enormously long fourth finger on each hand, and anchored to their hind legs. The other front claws were short and hooked, probably useful for crawling and clinging.

Bones and Brains

Pterosaurs were not the ancestors of birds, but they both had hollow bones, which helped to lighten their bodies and so enable them to fly. Their brains were also like those of birds, with a large cerebellum (the part controlling balance) and huge optic lobes to make them sharp-eyed. Probably, they breathed in the same way, too, but the soft parts that animals breathe with don't get fossilised and so we can't say for sure.

Fur or Feathers?

In 1970 a small fossil of a **pterosaur** was found in Russia that showed evidence of a thick coat of fur on the body, and extending over the wings. It is hard to see what fur could be for except to keep warm, and this has made scientists think hard about whether flying dinosaurs might have been warm-blooded. Feathers are good for keeping warm, too, and not a lot of use for flying until they are perfectly organized. If animals grew fur and feathers to keep warm, this must mean they had to keep warmth *in*, and so they must have been warm-blooded.

Pteranodon

A fossil of one of the last and greatest of the Pterosaurs was found in Kansas, North America. It weighted 18kg, and had a body about the size of a turkey's, with a wingspan of 7m. It had a long beak and a huge crest of bone on its head. **Pteranodon** seems to have lived like an albatross, flying far out to sea, scooping fish from the water.

Giant Vultures

The biggest flying animal of all time had a wingspan of more than 15 metres (50 feet), 4 times as wide as any living bird! Found in Texas in 1971, this reptile was named **Quetzalcoatlus** after the Mexican wind god, and it must truly have ruled the skies 150 million years ago. It probably fed on carrion, like vultures do today, using its long neck to dig deep into the bodies of dead dinosaurs. Its bones were as light as polystyrene.

Some of the first dinosaurs were the largest land animals ever to have walked the Earth, the **sauropods.** They were all plant eaters. At this time, there was a warm wet climate with plenty of rivers and stretches of water, ideal for the dinosaurs.

The **Brontosaurus** were so heavy, they could not travel far to hunt for food. As trees became established, they developed very long necks to reach this source of food. Their small head housed a tiny brain — the size of a walnut — so they can't have been too clever!

How Big?

The **sauropods** were huge:

	weight	length
Diplodocus	11 tonnes	26m
Apatosaurus	30 tonnes	21m
Brontosaurus	51 tonnes	19.8m
Brachiosaurus	100 tonnes	28m

Meal Times

When it wanted to eat, a **sauropod** would stretch out its long neck to pull up plants or shrubs from the river or lakeside. If it had to move, it did so very slowly. It ate only soft marsh and lake plants — scientists know this because fossils show the teeth were weak, with a small jaw bone.

Fossil Tree

The gingko tree is found mainly China and Japan today, and is a survivor of the age of the dinosaurs. The rich frond-like leaves of the gingko provided food for the plant-eating dinosaurs.

Enemies

Despite their huge size, these giant herbivores such as **Diplodocus** and **Brontosaurus** were preyed upon by the meat-eating dinosaurs, although they did not like the water, so the sauropods were safer there than on land.

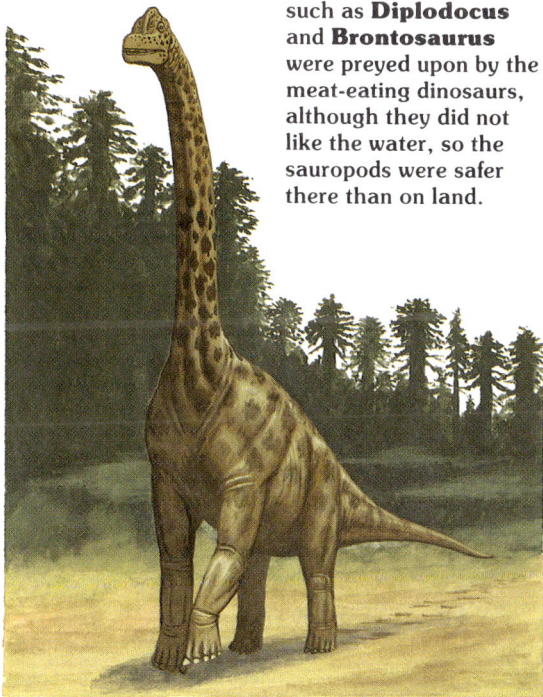

MEAT EATERS

Meat-eaters came first. Amphibians evolved from meat-eating fishes, and it was only after reptiles conquered the land that vertebrates began eating plants. And meat-eating dinosaurs were there already, waiting for them! Some hunted together in packs or groups; these were small and speedy, with sharp teeth and claws. Others were slow and bulky with huge jaws.

Megalosaurus

Megalosaurus was a meat eater. It was the first dinosaur whose fossils were studied, and the first to be named —

Megalosaurus means 'large lizard'. It lived about 140 million years ago, and its fossil bones were found in central and southern England by William Buckland in 1824.

Megalosaurus was extremely ferocious. It had a long mouth full of sharp teeth and a strong, thick neck full of powerful muscles. It was about 9m long and weighed 9 tonnes. The skull of a meat-eating dinosaur shows quite similar shaped teeth to the cheetah of today! The cheetah is a meat eater too.

Deinonychus

Deinonychus was one of the fastest, fiercest meat eaters. Its name means 'terrible claw', and it had a huge razor-sharp claw on its second toe which was 12cm long, and long arms with three-fingered clawed hands. **Deinonychus** was 4m long, and lived 120 million years ago in North America. It would leap on its victim, slashing with its claws, and using its long tail to balance — it may also have helped in steering around corners.

Allosaurus

Allosaurus was a very fierce dinosaur. It was a meat eater, and hunted other plant-eating dinosaurs. It stood on two legs and was 10m long. Its mouth opened so wide that it could swallow small animals whole.

Tiny Terror

The smallest dinosaur yet discovered was a creature barely 61cm (2 feet) long, which is called **Compsognathus.** It was a flesh-eater, as we can tell from its teeth, and looked very much like a bird. It may even have had feathers!

STEGOSAURUS

Stegosaurus lived 140-150 million years ago in the western United States and also in England. It was a very slow-moving animal, about 6m long.

Brainpower
Stegosaurus had the smallest brain of any animal compared to its size. It weighed nearly 2 tonnes, with a brain no bigger than a walnut, so it probably was not a very intelligent animal!

Armour
Stegosaurus was a plant eater. With many highly dangerous meat eaters roaming about, it needed good protection. It had a row of great bony plates along its back, and a big strong tail with four fierce sharp spikes on it. When the tail was swished to the side, it could easily cripple a small meat eater, and a blow from it could probably also have wounded a meat eater such as **Megalosaurus,** though bigger ones would not have been kept at bay for long.

Armour or Heating?

The double row of bony plates along **Stegosaurus's** back looks very fierce, but it did not protect the sides or legs at all. Some scientists think that the plates helped control its temperature — when the animal was too hot, they may have worked like a radiator, letting heat leave the body through the plates.

Warm or Cold?

Modern reptiles become sluggish when the temperature falls. The warmer they are, the faster they can move — within reason, of course! It is possible that a huge animal like **Stegosaurus** used those large plates to give it extra surface for heating and cooling, but what about the big dinosaurs that had no plates?

Central Heating

The term 'cold-blooded' isn't quite true. All living things make some heat, just because of the chemistry going on inside them. Even plants make heat — you can see how snow melts on grass faster than on bare ground. Deep inside a giant dinosaur's body the heat generated by chemistry must simply have built up, insulated from the cold outside by tonnes of flesh.

TWO-LEGGED PLANT EATERS

Hypsilophodon
Hypsilophodon was a very small dinosaur, only about 2.3m long. It lived 120 million years ago in Europe and North America.

Fastest Runners
Small, agile, plant-eating dinosaurs like **Hypsilophodon** were among the fastest runners — they probably needed to get away from predators!
By measuring their legs and comparing their shape to that of modern animals, experts have estimated that they could run as fast as 45kph.

Tree Dweller?
When **Hypsilophodon** was first discovered, it was thought to live in trees, because of its grasping toes and balancing tail. In fact, it was believed to be the dinosaur equivalent of a tree kangaroo that lives in Papua New Guinea today. Now this theory has been proved wrong; **Hypsilophodon** was a ground-dwelling dinosaur that used its stiff tail as a stabilizer while running.

Iguanodon

Iguanodon was a much larger plant eater, about 8m long, which also lived 120 million years ago in Europe. It stood on its back legs to feed, so that it could reach the tops of trees. It had a large sharp spike on each 'thumb'. Scientists believe that it used this spike to fight off its attackers — perhaps it drove the spike into the attacker's stomach or eye!

Iguanodon's tail was very thick and heavy, but it could lift it in order to run, and could sit back on it when tired!

Dinosaur Dinner

In 1854, dinosaur models were built for the Crystal Palace gardens in London. The sculptor actually made **Iguanodon** look more like a rhinoceros, and before finishing it he held a dinner party in it for 21 important scientists!

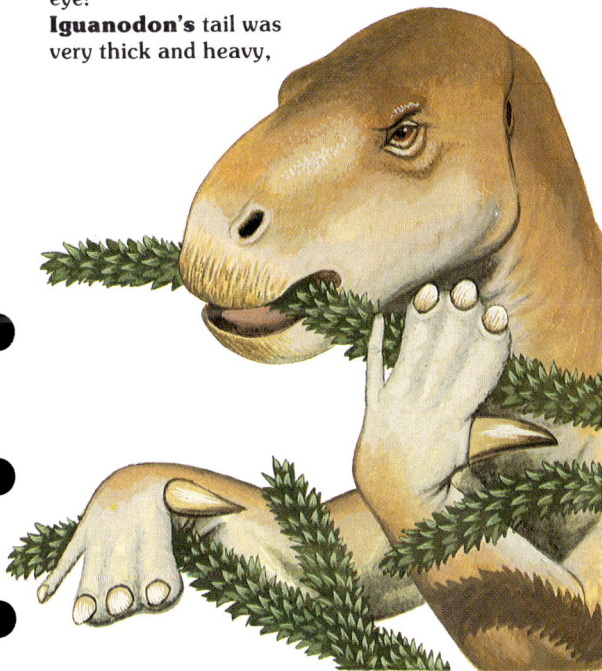

ARMOURED DINOSAURS

In some cases, dinosaur skin was armour-plated for extra protection. Bones were actually fused together to form a bony armour. These creatures were squat and very heavy. They looked rather like giant armadillos. They ate plants and protected themselves from large meat eaters by crouching, and clinging to the ground.

Early Armour

When dinosaurs evolved, armoured crocodile-like reptiles, such as **Desmatosuchus,** already existed. Turtles also evolved alongside dinosaurs. **Desmatosuchus** disappeared without trace, but turtles are still with us today.

Bony Spikes

Polacanthus was about 4m long and lived 120 million years ago, in Europe. Fossils of this creature were found on the Isle of Wight, in southern England! It was a four-legged animal, and was incredibly well armoured with a double row of sharp spikes running along its back. These, together with its overlapping bony plates along its tail, would have discouraged hungry meat eaters from attacking. Between the spikes, though, **Polacanthus** was still soft and meaty. Later on, its distant descendants grew much better armour.

Armoured Tanks

A new group of armoured dinosaurs evolved about 120 years ago. These were the **ankylosaurs,** which were squat, short-legged creatures whose skin was reinforced with bony plates that joined together to make a strong shell. These walking armoured tanks survived a long time, right up to the end of the Age of Dinosaurs.

Acanthopolis

Only a few specimens of this early **ankylosaur** have been found, in Southeast England. It was covered with bony plates, but lacked the spikes and knobs that later, more dramatic kinds were covered with.

Ankylosaurus

The whole group of **ankylosaurs** were named after the first one to be discovered. This 3-tonne beast was about 4.5m long, and was also covered with heavy bony plates all over its head, back and tail, which protected it from attack, like a suit of armour. At the end of the tail was a big lump of bone with spikes on it, which it could swing like a club to protect itself against enemies.

THE HADROSAURS

Some dinosaurs had most oddly shaped heads, and the most spectacular of these belonged to the **hadrosaurs,** or duckbills, so-called because of their broad beaks. They were the last and most successful of the two-legged plant-eating dinosaurs.

Feeding
Hadrosaurs had rows of small teeth, used for tackling tough vegetation from the trees. They had small webbed feet in front for swimming, and a pair of strong, larger legs at the back for walking or running. It is thought that they were mainly land-dwellers, probably living around the lakes and marshes.

Anatosaurus
Anatosaurus, or 'goose lizard', was about 12m long, and lived about 80 million years ago in North America. It had no crest on its head, but had a broad, duck-like beak. Inside its beak, there were more than 1000 teeth, in 60 rows on each jaw, arranged in 6 layers. These teeth enabled **Anatosaurus** to eat many of the new, tough flowering plants that were evolving.

Proof of the Pudding...

In 1922, the mummified (dried-up) remains of an **Anatosaurus** were found, with its last meal still in its stomach. Just before it died, it had fed on conifer-needles, seeds, twigs and fruit, crunched up between the grindstones of its jaws.

Bonehead
Pachycephalosaurus was the largest of a group of dinosaurs nicknamed 'boneheads' because of their thick skulls. These were up to 25cm thick, and may have acted like a crash helmet when they fought each other — real head-on collision!

Corythosaurus

This creature had a bony crest which looked rather like a helmet. This crest may have helped them to recognise each other. Other hadrosaurs had bizarre heads, too. Many reasons have been dreamed up for these strange crests, but the most likely explanation so far is that since they connected up with the animal's nose they gave it a superb sense of smell. Hadrosaurs had very good hearing, too, and might have lived in herds, like antelopes do today.

CERATOPSIANS

Another group of plant-eating dinosaurs were the horned dinosaurs, or **ceratopsians.** In fact, the earliest ceratopian had no horn, but it had a 'bump' on its snout which showed where the horn would develop in later animals.

Small Beginnings
Protoceratops (or 'first-horned face') was a smallish reptile, only 2m long, and about the height of a big dog. Later **ceratopsians** were much bigger. **Protoceratops** walked on all fours, and had a very heavy head with horns and a large collar like a frill on its neck. This shield was needed to strengthen the muscles of the neck and jaw so that they stayed attached to each other. It was also a display structure: the larger the frill, the larger and more powerful the adult. It had no teeth, but a horny beak, like that of tortoises and turtles. **Protoceratops** remains have been found all over the world.

Dinosaur Eggs
In Mongolia in the 1920s several fossilised nests of **Protoceratops** were found. These nests contained eggs, young reptiles and adults. The eggs were about 20cm long. Eggs of nine different dinosaurs have so far been found; the biggest is 30cm long, and would have held 5½ pints — twice as much as an ostrich egg.

Triceratops

This was the biggest of all the **ceratopsians,** weighing up to 5 tonnes, and measuring up to 9m long! It had three horns, two on top of its head and one on its nose. The head horns were 90cm long. These horns were mainly to defend itself against **tyrannosaurs,** but also were used in one-to-one combat — the male **Triceratops** would lock horns with another and head wrestle, just like deer, antelope and sheep do today.

Triceratops seems to have had a huge appetite — it ate plants and the trunks of trees like a bulldozer and munched them to a pulp with its teeth, of which it had 35 in each jaw. If one of its teeth wore down, it simply grew another one!

Styracosaurus

Styracosaurus or 'spiked lizard' was one of the bigger **ceratopsians.** It lived 75 million years ago in North America, and was about 5m long. It looked fierce but ate plants, not animals. It had a beak like a parrot's and a frill which was formed into spikes. This gave it extra protection against an attack on its neck.

FIERCE-LOOKING BEASTS

Tyrannosaurus Rex

The 'terrible tyrant king' of the dinosaurs lived in Mongolia and North America some 70 million years ago. It was about 12m long, weighed about 7 tonnes and had 23cm-long claws on its three-toed feet. It was about 6m high, so even a really tall human being would reach only to **Tyrannosaurus's** knees! It had a massive head, and the enormous mouth was full of dagger– and saw-like teeth. Each tooth was about 15cm long. It had very short front legs and tiny hands, with only two claws, so it could not even bring its hands up to its mouth. Its brain was very small for its body size.

Tyrannosaurus Rex was the largest carnivore that has ever lived on land, and was the most savage and blood-thirsty of them all!

Stones
Tyrannosaurus Rex often used to stuff itself full and then swallow large stones to help its digestion. There was only one time when it was not incredibly dangerous — when it had had a large meal. Then **Tyrannosaurus** might sleep for two weeks!

Other Tyrannosaurs
Although **T. rex** is the biggest of its kind yet discovered, it is not the only one. At least two others have been unearthed, one in Mongolia called **Tarbosaurus** and another in N. America called **Gorgosaurus.** They share the short front legs, massive head and sharp teeth of **T. rex,** and may have been better hunters because they were smaller.

'Terrible Hand'
Deinonychus was a savage hunter, although it only stood 1 metre high. Where **tyrannosaurs** were merely equipped to rend flesh, this meat-eater was armed with sharp talons that it clearly used for killing! In 1965, in the Gobi Desert of Mongolia, a pair of huge forearms were found that were similar to those of **Deinonychus** — but four times the size! If this animal, which has been named **Deinocheirus** — 'terrible hand', was what we think it might have been, then it would have been more terrible by far than any **tyrannosaur!**

THE LAST DINOSAURS

Dinosaurs roamed the Earth for nearly 150 million years. **Monoclonius** and six **Triceratops** were some of the last dinosaurs to appear before they all vanished completely from the Earth. They were both **ceratopsians,** or horned dinosaurs, and moved on all fours and were stocky, like the rhinoceroses of today; both were plant eaters.

Hadrosaurs
At the end of the dinosaur heyday, many of the creatures roaming the world were hadrosaurs, crested, duck-billed creatures with excellent senses of hearing, vision and smell as well as useful hands.

Pterosaurs
When the dinosaur age ended, the skies were ruled by flying dinosaurs of all shapes and sizes, from sparrow-sized little insect-eaters to great soaring dinosaur-vultures. Like **Hadrosaurs,** they were a very successful group of creatures.

Flourishing

Other dinosaurs that seemed to be doing well included the armoured **ankylosaurs,** giant **iguanodons,** and the egg eating **orinthomimids.**

Flesh-eaters

As well as big plant-eaters, the meat-eaters like **tyrannosaurs** and other **carnosaurs** ('meat lizards') that fed on them also lived right up to the end.

Where Are They Now?

Of all the wonderful dinosaurs that lived so long and so successfully, only one group is still alive today. Unlikely as this may seem, the birds are the only living true descendants from the dinosaurs. However, crocodiles — our own ferocious reptiles — are the last survivors of the **archosaurs**, the sub-class which included dinosaurs and other groups.

RECORD BREAKERS

Fastest
Gallimimus was one of the fastest dinosaurs. It was remarkably bird-like, with a toothless beak. Its hands were not adapted for grasping. It could run up to 55kph, almost as fast as a racehorse.

Smallest
Compsognathus was one of the smallest dinosaurs — it was a nimble, fast-running predator. Its head was 7.6cm long, and it was no heavier than a cat — about the size of a cockerel. As it was so small it could run very fast on its two back legs, and pursued lizards, frogs and other small creatures.

Longest Neck
Mamenchisaurus, found in China, had a neck 10m long, probably the longest neck of all the dinosaurs. It did not have a very long tail to balance the neck.

Tallest
Ultrasaurus, a sauropod, is thought to be the tallest of the dinosaurs. It stood 18m high, as high as 20 large elephants!

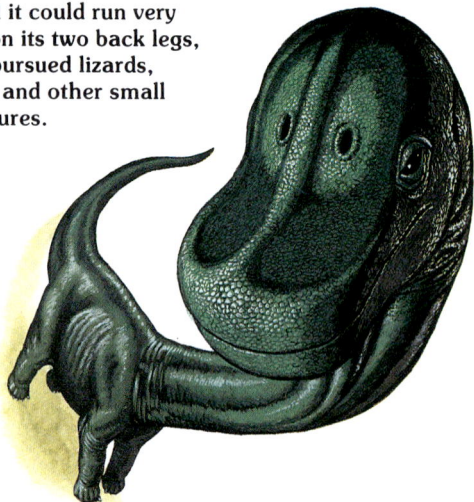

Smallest Brain

Stegosaurus had one of the smallest brains in proportion to its size — its brain was the size of a walnut. This creature may not have been as stupid as it might appear, as it did manage to survive for over 10 million years!

Largest Flying

The giant **Quetzalcoatlus,** with a wingspan of up to 15m, holds not only the record for largest flying dinosaur, but largest flying creature of all time!

Heaviest

The heaviest dinosaur, as calculated from a complete skeleton, was a **Brachiosaur** from Tanzania, which is thought to have weighed 78 tonnes when it was alive. An astounding fact about **Brachiosaurs** is that their legs were so strong that they could have supported their whole gigantic body on one leg without it breaking! Until scientists worked this out, it was believed that these plant-eaters needed water to help them stand.

Longest

The longest dinosaur was **Diplodocus,** a giant plant-eater that lived about 150 million years ago. In the Carnegie Museum in Pittsburgh, Pennsylvania, there is a skeleton of one of these beasts that measures 26.6m from end to end.

Cleverest

Stenonychosaurus was probably the cleverest dinosaur. It used its intelligence to outwit small, fast prey.

PREHISTORIC TIME

(Each number refers to millions of years ago.)

2	**First humans**
27	**Earliest apes**
55	**Mammals**
65	**Dinosaurs die out**
140	**First birds**
190	**First mammals**
210	**First dinosaurs**
300	**First reptiles**
345	**First amphibians**
380	**First insects**
400	**First land plants**
450	**The first fish**
4600	**The Earth is formed**

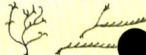

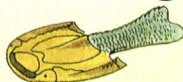

First civilisations

DINOSAURS DISAPPEAR

The dinosaurs ruled the Earth for over 220 million years, when something peculiar happened. Within only a few thousand years, they died out. Almost all at once the enormous plant- and meat-eating land animals, the huge flying reptiles and the sea beasts became extinct. Only a few reptiles were left — crocodiles, lizards, snakes, tortoises and turtles. There are several theories as to what caused this; it was probably a combination of them all.

Change of Climate

Dinosaurs lived in a warm, wet, steamy climate. Plants grew all the year round as the weather did not change. This suited the plant eaters, and so too the carnivorous dinosaurs! Around 60-75 million years ago the climate began to be more variable, or seasonal. Some trees began to lose their leaves in winter, letting the plant-eating dinosaurs go hungry.

Land Movement

At this time, there was a lot of land movement on Earth. The continents became separated by wide stretches of sea. As a result, much of the low lying land where dinosaurs lived was left high and dry. Oceans became deeper, land became higher, drier and colder. The giant plant-eaters depended on lush tropical vegetation, which wasn't to be found either in the now-deep ocean waters or on the dry, increasingly cold and mountainous land. Without plant-eaters to feed on, flesh-eaters would also go hungry.

Smokescreen

It has been suggested that some really big catastrophe happened on Earth around 65 million years ago. For example, if a giant asteroid crashed into our planet it could make such a mess that millions of tonnes of dust must get into the atmosphere. This would blot out the sun, perhaps for hundreds of years, and cause darkness that would kill all the plants.

Volcanoes

Big volcanic eruptions throw up dust into the atmosphere. In modern times, the fall in the Earth's temperature, though small, has been enough to measure after a really big eruption. There is not enough evidence yet, though, to support such dramatic theories as space-crashes or monster volcanoes.

Did They Fail?

It is sometimes said that dinosaurs 'died out' because they weren't good enough. They were good enough to survive for over 200 million years, though, and we've only been around for a hundredth of that time, so we've not beaten them yet!

THE FIRST BIRDS

Birds did not evolve from flying dinosaurs **(pterosaurs).** Their ancestors were probably little dinosaurs that ran on two legs, but nobody has found the 'missing link'. **Compsognathus,** the smallest known dinosaur, looks very like a bird without wings. Feathers most probably came first as a way of keeping warm, and were only later used for flight. The trouble with feathers is that they don't make good fossils, so we don't know when they first evolved!

Archaeopteryx
The earliest-known animal with feathers lived 140 million years ago, at the time of the dinosaurs, and was called **Archaeopteryx,** which means 'ancient feather'. In 1861, workmen in a German limestone quarry found the fossil impression of a single feather in the rock layer where many fossil reptile remains had been found. A fossil skeleton was found soon after. It looked like that of a small reptile with a long bony tail, but had feathers and a wishbone like a bird, and was the size of a small pigeon. It had teeth, not a beak. Scientists have now agreed that

Archaeopteryx could not really fly, as it did not have strong flight muscles or a well-developed brain. It may have used its wings to glide from branch to branch of trees.

Archaeopteryx, which had both reptile and bird features, may have been a step in the evolution of dinosaurs to birds.

Ichthyornis

The 'fishbird' was rather more like modern birds. It had well developed wings and was a strong flyer. About 20cm tall, **Ichthyornis** may have been an ancient gull, although its upper jaw probably had teeth as well as a beak.

Hesperornis

This was the earliest known true bird. It was a huge sea bird with no wings, and it lived about 80 million years ago. It was 2m long, with webbed feet. It had only one bone in its arm, so it could not have flown, but was a very good swimmer.

MAMMALS

What Are Mammals?

Mammals are warm-blooded animals, which means they are able to keep their body temperature about the same, whatever the outside temperature. They have fur or hair, not scales like the reptiles, and feed their babies with their own milk.

The earliest mammals lived alongside the dinosaurs. They were small, like **Phascolotherium,** and ate insects or seeds. When the dinosaurs died out, mammals had the world to conquer. Over millions of years they became more numerous, and much bigger!

Uintatherium was present 30 million years after the dinosaurs died out. It was a plant eater, 3.6m long, as big as an elephant.

The First Horse

At this time, **Eohippus** was alive — it was the earliest ancestor of the horses and zebras on Earth today. Only 30cm high, it lived on the grassy plains, and needed to run fast to escape from predators. **Eohippus** had toed feet, each toe ending in a small hoof.

Marsupials

As large pieces of the Earth moved over millions of years, some areas were cut off — in Australia, which was never in contact with any other continent, the marsupials evolved. A marsupial carries its young around in a pouch. The kangaroo and koala are today's marsupials.

Paraceratherium

The largest land mammal that has ever lived was 8.2m tall, and lived in Asia about 35 million years ago. It ate leaves from the treetops, like giraffes do today.

Diprotodon, a huge prehistoric wombat was a relative of the koala. **Procoptodon** was a huge kangaroo: it was over 3m tall.

THE GREAT ICE AGE

The climate was favourable to these huge mammals for millions of years, until the Earth started to become cooler — rivers froze, north winds blew persistently and many mammals died out. Animals able to cope with cold evolved, like the woolly **mammoth,** an elephant with a hairy coat and huge tusks. These tusks were used to shovel snow off the grass which it ate.

Man

When the world became warmer again, as it came out of the Ice Ages, these animals probably became extinct. Humans are related to the apes, and the first known ape, **Aegyptopithecus,** was present 27 million years ago in Egypt. Modern man did not develop until much later so we have had a very short lifespan compared to the dinosaurs!